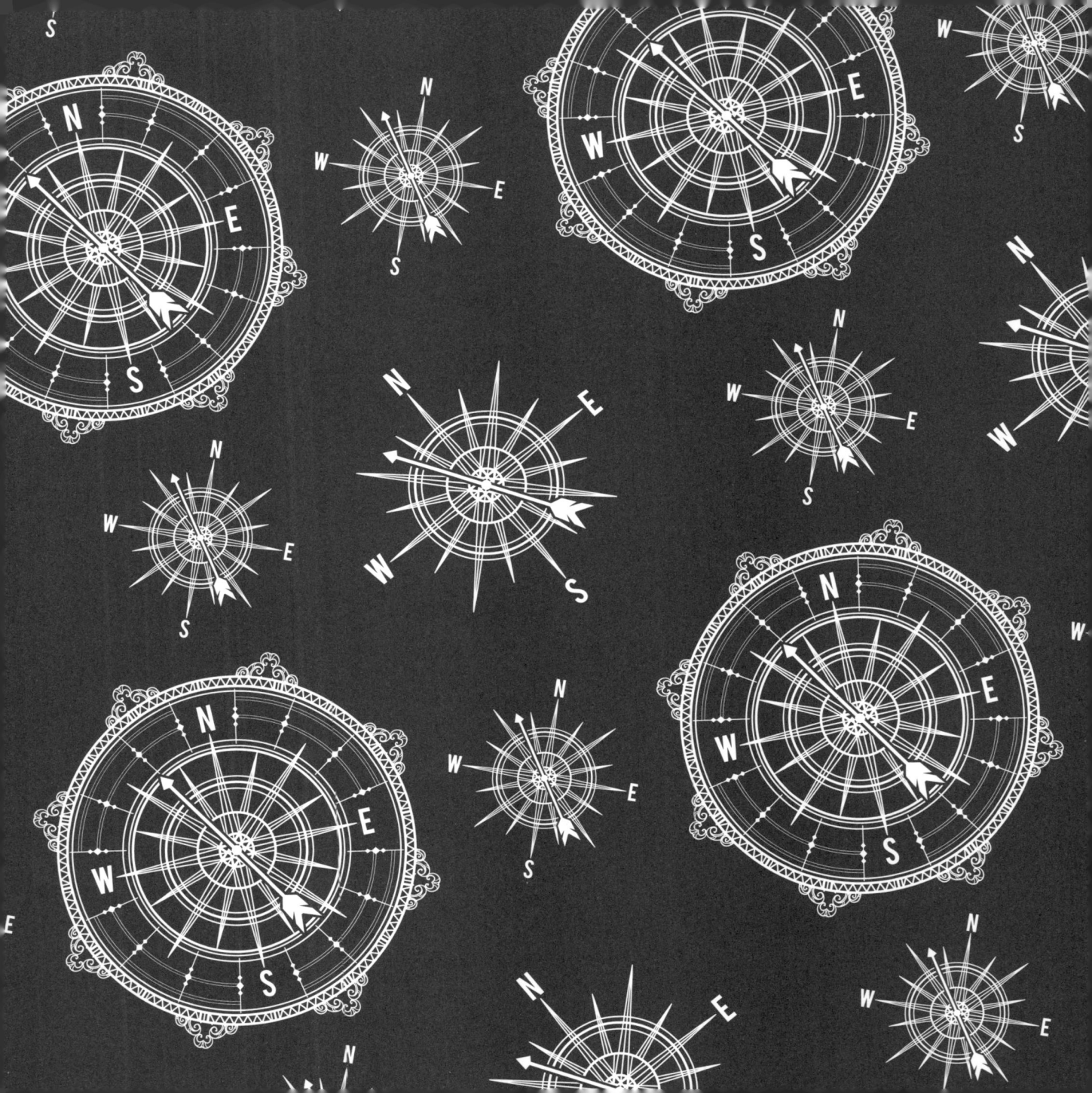

FOR THE LOVE OF BOATS

Dedication

To the Great Rondini,
Ron Sellers Senior, Seagoing Marine,
Scoutmaster extraordinaire, dedicated father,
and inexhaustible source of almost-funny one-liners.

Published by Sellers Publishing, Inc.
Copyright © 2020 Sellers Publishing, Inc.
Illustrations © 2020 Peter Scott
All rights reserved.

Sellers Publishing, Inc.
161 John Roberts Road, South Portland, Maine 04106
Visit our website: www.sellerspublishing.com • E-mail: rsp@rsvp.com

Charlotte Cromwell, Production Editor

ISBN 13: 978-1-5319-1208-6

Endpapers illustration © 2020 Nikolayenko Yekaterina/www.shutterstock.com

No portion of this book may be reproduced, stored in a
retrieval system, or transmitted in any form or by any means,
mechanical, electronic, photocopying, recording, or otherwise,
without the written permission of the publisher.

10 9 8 7 6 5 4 3 2 1

Printed in China.

FOR THE LOVE OF BOATS

A Well-Built Boat Is a Joy to Behold

Ronnie Sellers *with illustrations by Peter Scott*

Schooner

Introduction

As its title suggests, this is a book that was created for those who love boats.

As a species, our relationship with the water is primal. We came from it. We are, for the most part, made of it. We derive sustenance from it. We are inspired by it.

It is impossible to know for certain when one of our distant ancestors launched the first vessel and ventured forth onto the water. Recorded history simply does not reach back that far.

What motivated the first mariner to embark upon that virgin voyage? Perhaps it was the need for sustenance; there were more fish to be caught offshore than close to the beach. Perhaps it was safety; the need to flee from a predator or an enemy. Or perhaps it was inspired by some deeper metaphysical need; the need to venture forth and discover new places, go where no one else had gone, test one's courage, resourcefulness, and physical capabilities.

No matter what type of boat was used and what motivated that first voyage, it's likely the first mariner felt a thrill when floating on top of the water rather than in it, and, like every other mariner to follow, developed a deep appreciation . . . perhaps even a love . . . for the vessel that buoyed him up and carried him off to parts previously unknown. This love is one I, and millions of other boaters, understand.

My own fascination with boats began when I was ten years old. Early one warm Saturday morning in May, my best friend and I hiked down to Darby Creek, which ran through the forest behind our housing development in the suburbs of Philadelphia. The creek was swollen with the rushing waters of the spring thaw. We walked along the bank until we came to a sharp bend in the creek. There, on the other side of the bend from where we stood, was a raft that had been swept downstream by the strong current and deposited on a pile of rocks. It was a fairly small raft, crudely crafted from saplings lashed together with heavy hemp twine, but in our eyes it was a thing of beauty!

One remembers his or her first boat as vividly as one remembers a first kiss. We stood staring at the raft, our minds swirling as we imagined the many adventures it would make possible, and although we both knew it would be risky to launch it in the rough rushing creek waters, we pushed it down the rocks to the water's edge, cut a couple of poles with our pen knives so we'd have something to steer it with, and shoved off.

The voyage was as brief as it was exhilarating. We whooped and hollered as we were swept out into the middle of the creek, whooshed around the bend, and then cascaded down into a calm, lake-like pool off to the side of the main flow. We high-fived each other and wondered out loud if we could make it to the Delaware River by nightfall. Our question was answered a few moments later when the current suddenly increased and pulled us back out to the center of the stream and into some rapids.

The rapids tested, then tore apart the lashings holding the raft together. Our craft disintegrated beneath us within seconds and we had to swim to shore. We sat on the rocks and watched as the logs that had formed the deck of our raft shot up into the air one by one and disappeared down the river. We were wet, cold, and shaken, but we had both learned two important lessons. Boating is great fun. Boating is dangerous.

As brief as that first voyage was, it lasted long enough to plant a seed in both of us. We spent every spare moment during the next few years on Darby Creek, poling, paddling, and sailing anything we could find that would float, from an old diving board that had been discarded by the local country club to a long flat aluminum tub with upturned ends that had been used to mix mortar and then left behind on a construction site. The older we got, the farther down the creek we ventured, and the more we realized how exhilarating being out on the water can be.

Years later, after graduating from college, I moved to a coastal town in the state of Maine. I quickly learned that in Maine, well-built boats of all types are highly valued, and the skilled craftspeople that build them are among the state's most valued and respected artisans. "Maine built boat" has been synonymous with superior workmanship and seaworthiness for hundreds of years. There are also other regions in the United States, the Pacific Northwest, the Chesapeake Bay, North Carolina, and Florida among them, and other cities and places around the world, known for their superior marine craftsmanship. What all of these boatbuilding regions have in common is a tradition of placing a high value on the design, construction, and performance of the boats that are built there.

Just as I'm quite sure every mariner remembers his or her first boat, I know that dedicated mariners share an interest in boats of all types . . . which brings me to what inspired this book. I was given a copy of a book titled *Notable Boats*, written by Nic Compton and illustrated by an artist named Peter Scott. The book includes descriptions and illustrations of thirty-six (named) vessels, each of which completed a noteworthy voyage or won a race that made maritime history. I thoroughly enjoyed reading the book and viewing Peter Scott's illustrations.

After reading *Notable Boats*, I contacted Peter and asked him if he would be interested in illustrating a book that featured a variety of types of boats; simple self-propelled boats, sailboats, workboats, historical boats, recreational boats. Peter was excited by the idea and we began building the list of boats that would be included.

While Peter was sketching, and then completing, his boat illustrations, I began to comb through files full of quotations and musings about boats and boating that I'd collected over the years. Often these came from well-known mariners and boat builders, but just as often the sources were famous writers, musicians, and public figures for whom boating had special meaning. I began to pair these with Peter's illustrations as he sent them to me. The idea was to balance Peter's visually inspiring drawings with writing that was also inspirational.

Every boater will agree with me, I'm sure, when I say that a well-built boat is a joy to behold. The same is true, in my opinion, about Peter Scott's carefully researched and well-rendered illustrations of boats.

If the reader finds joy within the pages of this book, and perhaps learns a thing or two while perusing it, then Peter and I shall have achieved our objective, which was to create a book to inspire those who readily admit their lives would be less happy if it weren't for the love of boats.

Ronnie Sellers

Self Propelled Boats

We drag at oars with aching arms, and suddenly a puff of wind, a puff faint and tepid and laden with strange odors of blossoms, of aromatic wood, comes out of the still night — the first sigh of the East on my face. That I can never forget. It was impalpable and enslaving, like a charm, like a whispered promise of mysterious delight.

Joseph Conrad,
Youth

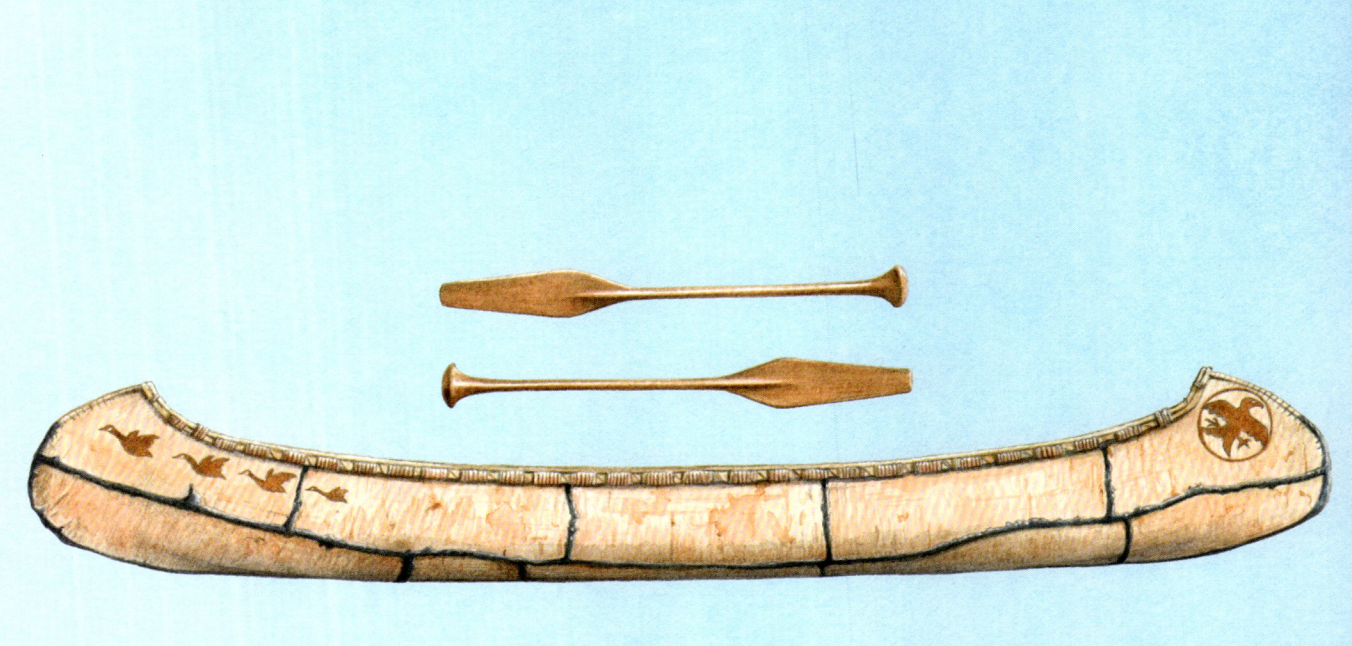
Birch Bark Canoe

The vessel in which Cap and his niece had embarked for their long and adventurous journey was one of the canoes of bark which the Indians are in the habit of constructing, and which, by their exceeding lightness and the ease with which they are propelled, are admirably adapted to a navigation in which shoals, flood-wood, and other similar obstructions so often occur.

James Fenimore Cooper,
The Pathfinder

Native Americans in the northeast built carefully crafted canoes using the bark from birch trees, primarily, for the sides and cedar for the framework. The bark of the birch tree grows laterally, which allowed it to be wrapped around the canoe's frame relatively easily. The canoes varied in size depending upon what they were being used for, but all were light enough to be carried easily and sturdy enough to withstand frequent collisions with rocks and other flotsam.

As he gained distance from the land, the ocean swelled with increasing volume. His frail skin kayak was lifted high on the oily crests of waves, and as it descended with swift rushes, Ootah felt exultant thrills in his heart.

T. Everett Harré,
The Eternal Maiden

The *kayak* is a vessel that has played a key role in North American arctic societies for thousands of years. It was designed to be fast, maneuverable and seaworthy, yet light enough to be carried easily by one person. Frames made from driftwood and bone were wrapped with the skins of mammals sewn together with rawhide and sinew, then waterproofed using animal fat. Seal bladders tucked inside added buoyancy. Bladders were also attached to harpoon lines to allow them to be retrieved. The fact that kayaks are among the most popular watercraft used by outdoor enthusiasts today is testimony to the brilliance of their design.

Kayak

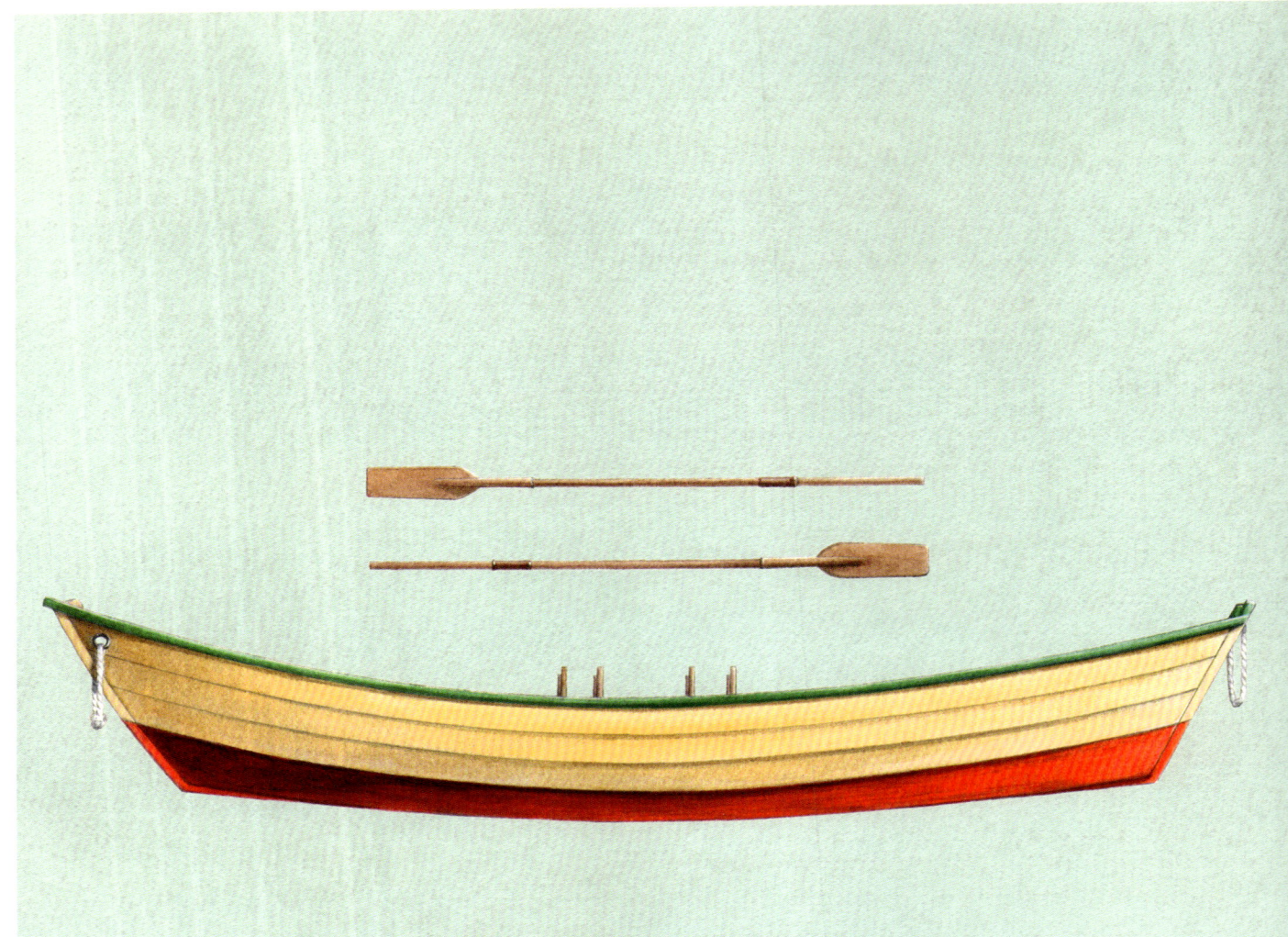

Grand Banks Dory

From every boat dories were dropping away like bees from a crowded hive, and the clamor of voices, the rattling of ropes and blocks, and the splash of the oars carried for miles across the heaving water.

Rudyard Kipling,
Captains Courageous

The *Grand Banks Dory* is a rugged rowboat, usually between 16 and 20 feet in length, that has been used along the Atlantic coast of the United States and Canada for fishing and general boating for hundreds of years. The sides of the dory are made from sturdy clinker built planks. The bottom of the boat is flat, enabling it to sit upright on the beach or on the bottom when the tide recedes. Both the bow and stern are raised, and the stern has a narrow transom. The thwarts are often removable, allowing the boat to be stacked. The Grand Banks Dory is not particularly stable in the water until it is loaded with passengers, cargo, or fish.

One takes what the river offers, both good and bad. The joy of living by running water far outweighs the sorrow.

Matthew Goldman,
The Journals of Constant Waterman:
Paddling, Poling, and Sailing for the Love of It

A *punt* is a flat-bottomed, shallow draft boat with a squared off bow and stern. It is propelled with a pole. Punts have been used for centuries on the rivers and fens of England, originally for transporting freight and for fishing and duck hunting, and later for recreation. Punting is still a favorite pastime on the river Cam in Cambridge and the river Thames in Oxford.

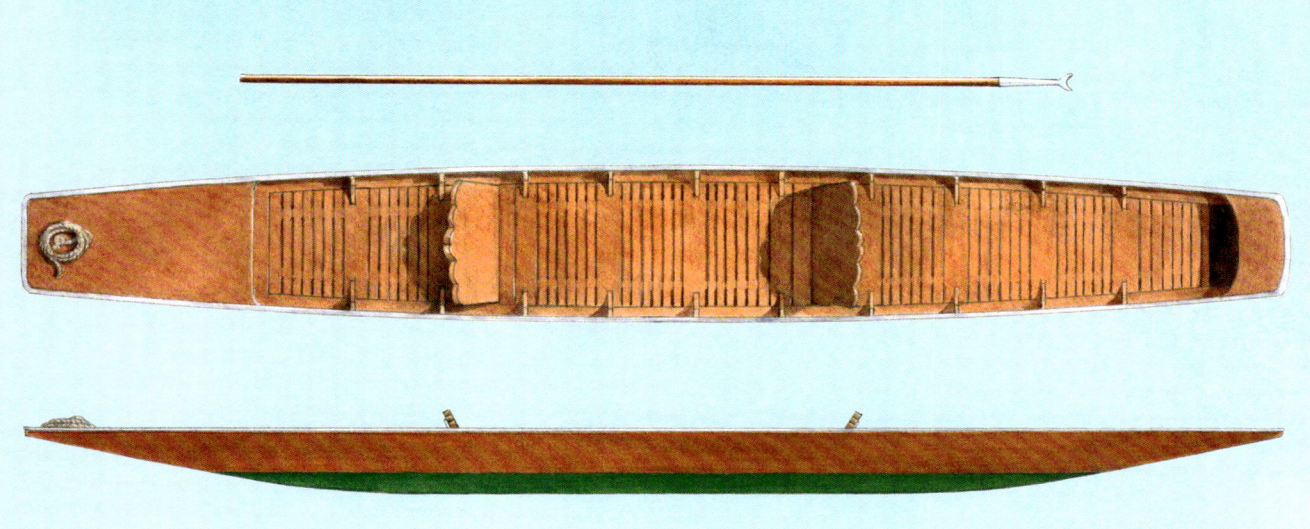

Punt

Cornish Pilot Gig

*Only the guy who isn't rowing
has time to rock the boat.*

Jean-Paul Sartre

The *Cornish Pilot Gig* is a relatively long wooden rowboat (32 feet) that is propelled by six oarsmen, each of whom pulls one oar. They were originally used as lifeboats and to transport pilots out to ships. Today racing pilot gigs is a popular sport in England and elsewhere, overseen by the Cornish Pilot Gig Association.

> *. . . . But there the Duke was given to understand*
> *That in a gondola were seen together*
> *Lorenzo and his amorous Jessica.*
>
> William Shakespeare,
> *The Merchant of Venice, Act 2, Scene 8.*

The unique profile of this handmade, meticulously constructed wooden rowboat is iconic, and conjures up thoughts of idyllic cruises through the canals of Venice. The *gondola* has a flat bottom, is approximately 35 feet in length, lists slightly to offset the powering stroke of the gondolier, and is, by regulation, painted black. The decorative metal prow, called a "ferro," helps to counter-balance the weight of the gondolier as he rows, and helps to protect the boat against damage.

Gondola

Sailboats

Sailing a boat calls for quick action, a blending of feeling with the wind and water as well as with the very heart and soul of the boat itself. Sailing teaches alertness and courage, and gives in return a joyousness and peace that but few sports afford.

George Matthew Adams

Being on a boat that's moving through the water, it's so clear. Everything falls into place in terms of what's important and what's not.

James Taylor

The *Peapod* was a boat designed in the late 19th century for lobster fishing along the coast of Maine. They could be sailed or rowed, and their shallow draft and rugged plank-on-plank construction enabled them to be maneuvered in and around rocky shorelines relatively safely. Peapods were also quite stable, allowing lobstermen to lean over to one side of the boat while pulling up a trap without the boat taking on water.

Peapod

Catboat

Choose a modest, simple yacht — one you can afford and still have money in the bank. If you choose a yacht you can handle easily, you'll get out sooner and find real cruising comfort, mental and physical.

Lin & Larry Pardey,
Cruising In Seraffyn

Catboats were once the most popular and commonly used boats for fishing and general maritime purposes along the eastern seaboard of the United States. Their distinctive characteristics are a single mast set far forward, relatively low freeboard, a centerboard, a wide beam (as much as half as wide as the boat is long), and a four-sided gaff rigged sail (although modern catboats sometimes utilize a single marconi rig). They are slow in the water but sturdy, and capable of carrying a great deal of weight for their size.

A man can pretend to be a lot of things in this world, but he can only pretend to be a sailor for as long as it takes to clear the harbor mouth!

Bernard Hayman

Friendship sloops were first built in the town of Friendship, Maine, in the late 1800s. The shape of the hull was derived from that of the Muscongus Bay sloop, but with a deeper draft and a small cutty cabin forward. Whereas the Muscongus Bay sloop was used to fish in the shallows of the Maine coast, the Friendship sloop, with its increased length, heavier ballast and larger sail plan, was designed to enable fishermen to venture farther offshore to Georges Bank.

Friendship Sloop

Hereshoff Sloop

The cabin of a small yacht is truly a wonderful thing; not only will it shelter you from the tempest, but from the other troubles in life it is a safe retreat.

L. Francis Herreshoff

A *sloop* is the most popular configuration for contemporary sailors. It consists of a main mast positioned about 1/3 of the way aft of the bow for the main sail and a head sail. The large main sail combined with the headsail allows a sloop to perform well both upwind and downwind.

As soon as I get on my boat, something inside me changes. Then I really feel what living is.

Laura Dekker,
who, at sixteen, became the youngest person to circumnavigate the world

A *Yawl* is a sailboat with two masts. The aft (mizzen) mast is markedly smaller than the main mast, and is located behind the rudder post. The mizzen sail is used more for steering and stability than for power.

Yawl

Ketch

I am a citizen of the most beautiful nation on earth, a nation whose laws are harsh yet simple, a nation that never cheats, which is immense and without borders, where life is lived in the present. In this limitless nation, this nation of wind, light, and peace, there is no other ruler besides the sea.

Bernard Moitessier

A *ketch* is a sailboat with two masts. The mainmast is usually located about 1/3 of the way aft of the bow. The mizzenmast is further aft of the main, and shorter. The primary advantage of a ketch is the increased versatility the mizzen offers, especially in rough weather. Rather than reefing the main sail in high winds, the sailor can drop the main sail altogether and sail with just the jib and mizzen (referred to as sailing "jib and jigger").

We have Southern Ocean winds twenty-five knots from the west. Promise spreads her wings and glides with them. Day breaks with a spiritually fulfilling surprise, sunshine bursting through bright blue holes in the cloud cover. Oh, how I love the sight of the light in this sky, and I salute it aloud with a cheer.

Dodge Morgan,
The Voyage of American Promise

A *cutter* is a sailboat with a single mast. The mast is often positioned farther aft than that of a sloop. It is capable of flying up to five sails, but the most common sail plan includes a mainsail attached to the mast and boom, and a staysail and jib or genoa attached to the mast and the bowsprit or forestay. The ability to fly and/or furl more sails offers the mariner more control options, making it better able to contend with adverse conditions than a sloop. The fact that it only has one mast makes it lighter and easier to single-hand than a ketch or a schooner.

Cutter

Schooner

I really don't know why it is that all of us are so committed to the sea, except I think it's because in addition to the fact that the sea changes, and the light changes, and ships change, it's because we all came from the sea.... And when we go back to the sea — whether it is to sail or to watch it — we are going back from whence we came.

John F. Kennedy,
Remarks at the Dinner for the America's Cup Crews,
September 14, 1962

A *schooner* usually has two masts (sometimes more) positioned forward in the boat with the forward mast usually smaller than the aft mast. Forward of the foremast, a schooner can fly one or more jibs. Traditional schooners have gaff-rigged sails with a short spar (called a gaff) at the top, allowing the sails to extend back along the fourth side. This gives a larger sail area than a triangular sail of the same height.

Fishing & Working Boats

As proud as I am to be doing an interview,
or to be recognized as a best-selling author,
there's nothing that makes me prouder
than saying I'm a fisherman.

Linda Greenlaw,
Maine fishing boat captain

Bateau

Boats, like whiskey, are all good.

R.D. Culler

The early *Bateau* was designed with a contoured shallow-draft hull and high bow sheer that could pass over logs and debris in the bayous and still navigate streams and rivers with swift currents. Also referred to a "flats" boat or a "Johns" boat, it was, and still is, a favored form of transportation in south-central Louisiana.

> *The best boat to own is the one that will take you to where the fish are.*
>
> Captain Mike McCarty,
> *Fishing boat captain
> in the Dominican Republic*

Although *pangas* are arguably the most widely used boats in the world, the design is only about 50 years old. Where the design for the panga originated is the subject of much debate, but it's clear that the Baja area of Mexico is where the boats first proliferated. Later, The World Bank funded the manufacturing of Pangas in Central America, South America, the Caribbean, and elsewhere to enable third-world fisherman to have access to inexpensive, yet versatile and seaworthy vessels. Pangas are molded from fiberglass and have high-rise, flared bows, perfect for fishermen throwing nets to catch bait fish. Their shallow drafts (as little as 6 inches) allow them to access bays and rivers. Many have flotation along the gunwales for safety. Their narrow beams enable them to have sizeable outboard motors mounted onto them, and their sturdy V-shaped hulls allow them to be run right up onto the beach.

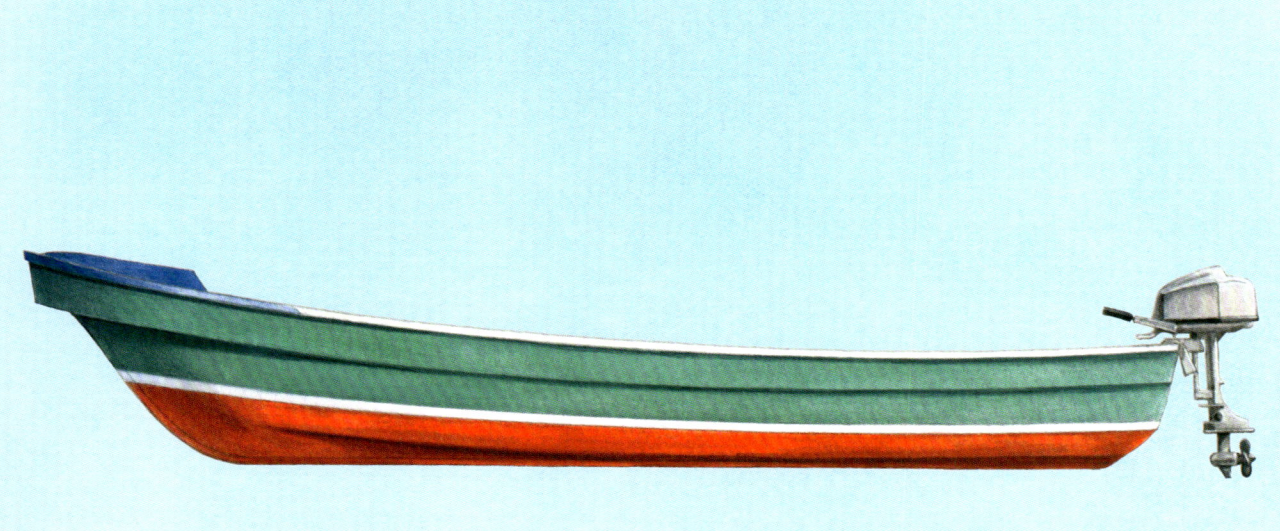

Panga

Downeast Maine Lobster Boat

At sea you need to maximize your control over everything that you can, to minimize the effects of those things you can't control, such as Mother Nature, who is known by all fishermen to be quite temperamental, and often a nuisance.

Linda Greenlaw,
The Hungry Ocean

With their sturdy semi-displacement hull, relatively wide beam, shallow draft and un-ballasted keel, *Downeast Maine lobster boats* are able to "tunk" up onto ledges without damage to the hull or running gear. These are workboats first and foremost, but they are often fitted out for recreational cruising by boaters who value their sturdiness and utility.

Shrimping gets in your heart, that's for sure. It's a love, like the first girl you meet when you're in high school. You fall in love with shrimping and there's nothing else. I can't imagine doing anything else.

Mack Liverman,
North Carolina shrimp boat captain

The silhouette of a *shrimp boat* heading with booms raised to or from the fishing grounds is unmistakable. When fishing, the booms are lowered and the nets attached to them dropped to drag along the sea bottom. A Turtle Exclusion Device in the trawl net allows sea turtles to escape unharmed. These boats have powerful engines, but their transmissions are designed to deliver high torque rather than speed.

Shrimp Boat

Chesapeake Bay Deadrise

The fishermen know that the sea is dangerous and the storm terrible, but they have never found these dangers sufficient reason for remaining ashore.

Vincent van Gogh

A high pointed bow that drops down at a steep angle to a long, flat cockpit with low gunwhales makes the silhouette of the *Chesapeake Bay Deadrise* as distinctive as it is functional. Popular among fishermen, crabbers, and oystermen who work the Chesapeake Bay, these shallow draft boats often feature a "draketail" (rounded) transom.

You have to be crazy to work on a tugboat, but if it gets in your blood then you're hooked for life.

Anthony Davis,
Tugboat Deckhand

Tugboats, with their relatively short length, broad beam and shallow draft, have been used for centuries to pull and push large ships up rivers and through harbors to their docks. Originally powered by steam and paddlewheels, most modern tugs utilize high-powered diesel engines and sophisticated propeller systems that maximize thrust and maneuverability.

Tugboat

Sportfishing Boat

> *"Perhaps I should not have been a fisherman,"*
> *he thought. "But that was the*
> *thing I was born for."*
>
> Ernest Hemingway,
> *The Old Man and the Sea*

During the first half of the 20th century, boat builders such as Rybovich, Whiticar and Merrit began producing powerboats specifically for sport fishing. Designed for deep sea big game fishing, these boats feature raised bows and foredecks, flybridges, and side sheers that break downward aft of the main cabin to enable fishermen to hoist their catches on board more easily. They are powered with large engines to enable the boat to reach, and return from, fishing grounds as quickly as possible. Outriggers, originally bamboo, are now aluminum. Many sportfishing boats also have aluminum towers attached to allow anglers to spot fish from afar.

Recreational Power Boats

Why do we love the sea? It is because it has some potent power to make us think things we like to think.

Robert Henri

Motor Launch

*The perfection of a yacht's beauty
is that nothing should be there
for only beauty's sake.*

John MacGregor

In the early 1900s, boat designers and builders produced wooden V-bottom *launches* powered by gasoline engines. These open boats were used by yacht clubs and marinas to transport owners and passengers to and from their moored vessels as well as for recreational purposes.

. . . There is nothing — absolutely nothing — half so much worth doing as simply messing about in boats.

Kenneth Grahame,
The Wind in the Willows

During the early and mid twentieth century, boat builders such as Gar Wood, Chris Craft, and Hacker produced exquisitely crafted *runabouts* for use on lakes and coastal waters. These boats were often made of mahogany, varnished to a mirror finish, and powered by the largest inboard engine that could fit inside their hulls. Collectors and enthusiasts have preserved and restored many of these boats, and they can still be seen today skipping across Lake Tahoe, Lake Michigan, Lake Winnipesaukee, Lake Como, and elsewhere.

Lake Runabout

Downeast Cruiser

Whenever I find myself growing grim about the mouth; whenever it is a damp, drizzly November in my soul . . . then, I account it high time to get to sea as soon as I can . . . . There is nothing surprising in this. If they but knew it, almost all men in their degree, some time or other, cherish very nearly the same feelings towards the ocean with me.

Herman Melville,
Moby Dick

The silhouette of the modern *Downeast cruiser* is reminiscent of the lobster boats that work the New England coast, but from a design standpoint they are more different than similar. The cruiser's planing hull is designed for speed while the lobster boat's semi-displacement hull sacrifices speed for stability. Most cruisers have wider transoms than their heavier cousins, lack a keel, and have hard chines versus the round chines more common on lobster boats. What they do have in common is a shallow draft, exceptional seaworthiness in almost all conditions, and beautiful lines!

Only two sailors, in my experience, never ran aground. One never left port and the other was an atrocious liar.

Don Bamford

Catamaran motor-powered cruising yachts were first manufactured by companies in Australia. Their two shallow draft hulls generate a minimal amount of resistance when moving through the water, allowing for greater speed and less fuel consumption per unit of power than mono-hull vessels. The broad beam also makes catamarans much less likely to capsize.

Catamaran

Indian Houseboat

*Land was created to provide
a place for boats to visit.*

Brooks Atkinson

In the Kerala state in southern India, elegant *houseboats* called Kettuvallam (boats held together by knots) ply the rivers and lagoons the area is famous for. These boats have been used for thousands of years, originally to carry freight and passengers. Now they transport tourists on holiday cruises. The hulls are made from planks held together with rope and caulked with coconut fiber and resin. The above deck structures are woven from all natural materials as well.

> *I bought a Dutch barge and turned it into a recording studio. My plan was to go to Paris and record while rolling down the Seine.*
>
> Pete Townshend

Canals are common throughout Europe, especially in England, Holland, and France, with some dating as far back as the 16th century. *Canal barges* were originally used to transport freight and were pulled, poled or sailed. Trains offered a more practical and expedient way to move freight, however, and now the canals of Europe are plied by luxury barges carrying tourists rather than cargo. The vessels offer every convenience and come complete with restaurant-quality galleys, elegant saloons, and bedroom suites. Narrow, long, and propelled by powerful diesel engines, these slow moving boats allow travellers to experience Europe in a unique and relaxing way.

French Canal Barge

Luxury Power Yacht

To the young Gatz, resting on his oars and looking up at the railed deck, the yacht represented all the beauty and glamor in the world.

F. Scott Fitzgerald,
The Great Gatsby

Beginning in the late 19th century, American boat builders such as Consolidated, Elco and, later, John Trumpy & Sons (builder of the Trumpy yacht Dovetail pictured here as well as the presidential yacht Sequoia), began to produce large, custom made luxury pleasure boats. These boats had thick wooden hulls and were designed to be capable of extended ocean cruising.

Classic & Historical Boats

It would be difficult to describe the subtle brotherhood of men that was here established on the seas. No one said that it was so. No one mentioned it. But it dwelt in the boat, and each man felt it warm him.

Stephen Crane,
The Open Boat

Polynesian Catamaran

It is not the ship so much as the skillful sailing that assures the prosperous voyage.

George William Curtis

Early mariners in India, Southeast Asia, and Malaysia developed double-hulled sailboats that were later adopted by other cultures and modified over time. Hulls got longer, enabling them to hold more weight, travel farther, and withstand the stresses of the open ocean. The hulls on the first *catamarans* were equal in size and made from hollowed out logs. Later on, boatbuilders reduced the size of one of the hulls to lighten the boat and increase speed and efficiency. Spars were laid across and lashed to the hulls with rope, then planks were attached to the spars to make a deck. Triangular "crab claw" sails were made from woven mats. Shelters made from small timbers and thatch and attached to the decking offered protection from the elements on long voyages.

For the most part, a sailboat navigates through its world of wind and water not leaving a single trace of its passage. Nothing is consumed. Nothing is altered. The winds and the water are left in exactly the same condition for the next user. Sailing is forever.

Michael B. McPhee

The native Uru people of Peru have built their boats using totora reed for hundreds of years. The reed, which grows plentifully in the Lake Titicaca area, is both buoyant, durable and easily fashioned.

Peruvian Reed Boat

Viking Longship

> *Leif set sail as soon as he was ready . . .*
> *and lighted upon lands of which*
> *before he had no expectation.*
>
> The Rev. J. Sephtone,
> *Erik the Red's Saga: a translation, 1880.*
> Description of Leif Erikson's first voyage

The seaworthiness of the longships built by the Norsemen is legendary. Hulls made from oak lapstrakes offered strength and flexibility sufficient to withstand the stresses of the open ocean during long voyages to Iceland, Greenland and beyond. The shallow draft of 2 feet or less allowed the Vikings to sail far inland on their raids. Shields fastened to the gunwales offered protection against both weather and the arrows of enemy archers. Sails woven from wool powered these sleek ships to speeds of up to 15 knots.

I was powerful glad to get away from the feuds, and so was Jim to get away from the swamp. We said there warn't no home like a raft, after all. Other places do seem so cramped up and smothery, but a raft don't. You feel mighty free and easy and comfortable on a raft.

Mark Twain,
The Adventures of Huckleberry Finn

Few things conjure up daydreams of escape, freedom, and adventure as readily as an image of a log raft floating on a river. This is as true today as it was more than a century ago when Mark Twain described how Huck Finn and Tom Sawyer felt when they first set sail on their raft down the Mississippi.

River Raft

Commuter Yacht

*Ah! The good old time — the good old time.
Youth and the sea. Glamor and the sea!
The good, strong sea, the salt, bitter sea,
that could whisper to you and roar at you
and knock your breath out of you.*

Joseph Conrad,
Youth

During the roaring 1920s and early 1930s, the scions of Wall Street had *commuter yachts* built for them to transport them from their homes on Long Island Sound to their offices on Wall Street. These wooden yachts were luxurious, sleek, and powered with engines large enough to allow them to reach speeds of 12 knots or more. The boat pictured here was built by the Consolidated Yacht Company in the late 1920s.

*Turn off your mind, relax,
and float downstream.*

John Lennon

Ornately decorated *Japanese Ferry* boats were originally built for, and used by, Japanese noblemen. Later, they became popular among wealthy businessmen and samurai as well who used them to cool down and relax out on the water during the warm summer months.

Japanese Ferry Boat

Chinese Junk

Twenty years from now, you will be more disappointed by the things you didn't do than those you did. So throw off the bowlines. Sail away from safe harbor. Catch the wind in your sails. Explore. Dream. Discover.

H. Jackson Browne

The *junk* is a sailing vessel that has been used in China for almost two thousand years. It has fully battened sails, and those used on rivers and in harbors had flat bottoms with daggerboards and a large stern-mounted rudder. The junk was the first vessel to be built with water-tight bulkheads that could be sealed off in the event that the hull was punctured.

Recommended Reading

Notable Boats, by Nic Compton, Illustrator Peter Scott,
Rizzoli International Publications, New York, 2017

Colin Archer and the Seaworthy Double-Ender, by John Leather,
Waterside Publications Ltd, Cornwall, England, 1995

Guide To Fitting Out, by Jim Emmett,
Ziff-Davis Publishing Company, New York, 1960

Wooden Boats: In Pursuit of the Perfect Craft at an American Boatyard,
by Michael Ruhlman,
Viking Penguin, New York, 2001

Origins of Sea Terms, by John G. Rogers,
Mystic Seaport Museum Inc, 1985

Captain James Cook, by Alan Villiers,
Charles Scribner's Sons, New York, 1967

Longitude: The True Story of a Lone Genius Who Solved the Greatest Scientific Problem of His Time, by Dava Sobel,
Walker and Company, Inc., 1995

Stories Of The Sea, Edited by Diana Secker Tesdell,
Alfred A. Knopf, New York, 2010

Gypsy Moth Circles the World, by Sir Francis Chichester,
Coward-McCann, Inc., New York, 1968

American Sailing Craft, by Howard I. Chapelle,
International Marine Publishing, Co., Camden, Maine, 1975

Pirates of the New England Coast 1630-1730,
by George Francis Dow and John Henry Edmonds,
Dover Publications, New York, 1996

Fifty Places to Sail Before You Die: Sailing Experts Share the World's Greatest Destinations, by Chris Santella,
Stewart, Tabori & Chang, New York, 2007

The Secret Life of Lobsters, by Trevor Corson,
Harper Collins, 2004

The Lore of Ships,
Crescent Books, New York, 1978

The Voyage of American Promise, Dodge Morgan,
Houghton Mifflin Harcourt, 1989

Godforsaken Sea: Racing the World's Most Dangerous Waters,
by Derek Lundy,
Algonquin Books of Chapel Hill, 1999

Visual Index

p. 14	p. 17	p. 18	p. 21	p. 22
Birch Back Canoe	Kayak	Grand Banks Dory	Punt	Cornish Pilot Gig
p. 25	p. 29	p. 30	p. 33	p. 34
Gondola	Peapod	Catboat	Friendship Sloop	Hereshoff Sloop
p. 37	p. 38	p. 41	p. 42	p. 46
Yawl	Ketch	Cutter	Schooner	Bateau

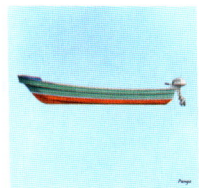
p. 49
Panga

p. 50
Maine Lobster Boat

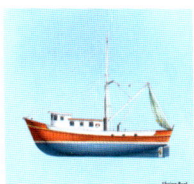
p. 53
Shrimp Boat

p. 54
Chesapeake Bay Deadrise

p. 57
Tugboat

p. 58
Sportfishing Boat

p. 62
Motor Launch

p. 65
Lake Runabout

p. 66
Downeast Cruiser

p. 69
Catamaran

p. 70
Indian Houseboat

p. 73
French Canal Barge

p. 74
Luxury Power Yacht

p. 78
Polynesian Catamaran

p. 81
Peruvian Reed Boat

p. 82
Viking Longship

p. 85
River Raft

p. 86
Commuter Yacht

p. 89
Japanese Ferry Boat

p. 90
Chinese Junk

About the Illustrator

Peter Scott uses traditional techniques of watercolor, ink, and gouache to create his award winning illustrations. More than forty of his solo books have been published worldwide.

As Peter is descended from a long line of master mariners and shipwrights, it is not surprising that boats are a favorite subject to paint. His studio is in an old sea captain's house overlooking the river.

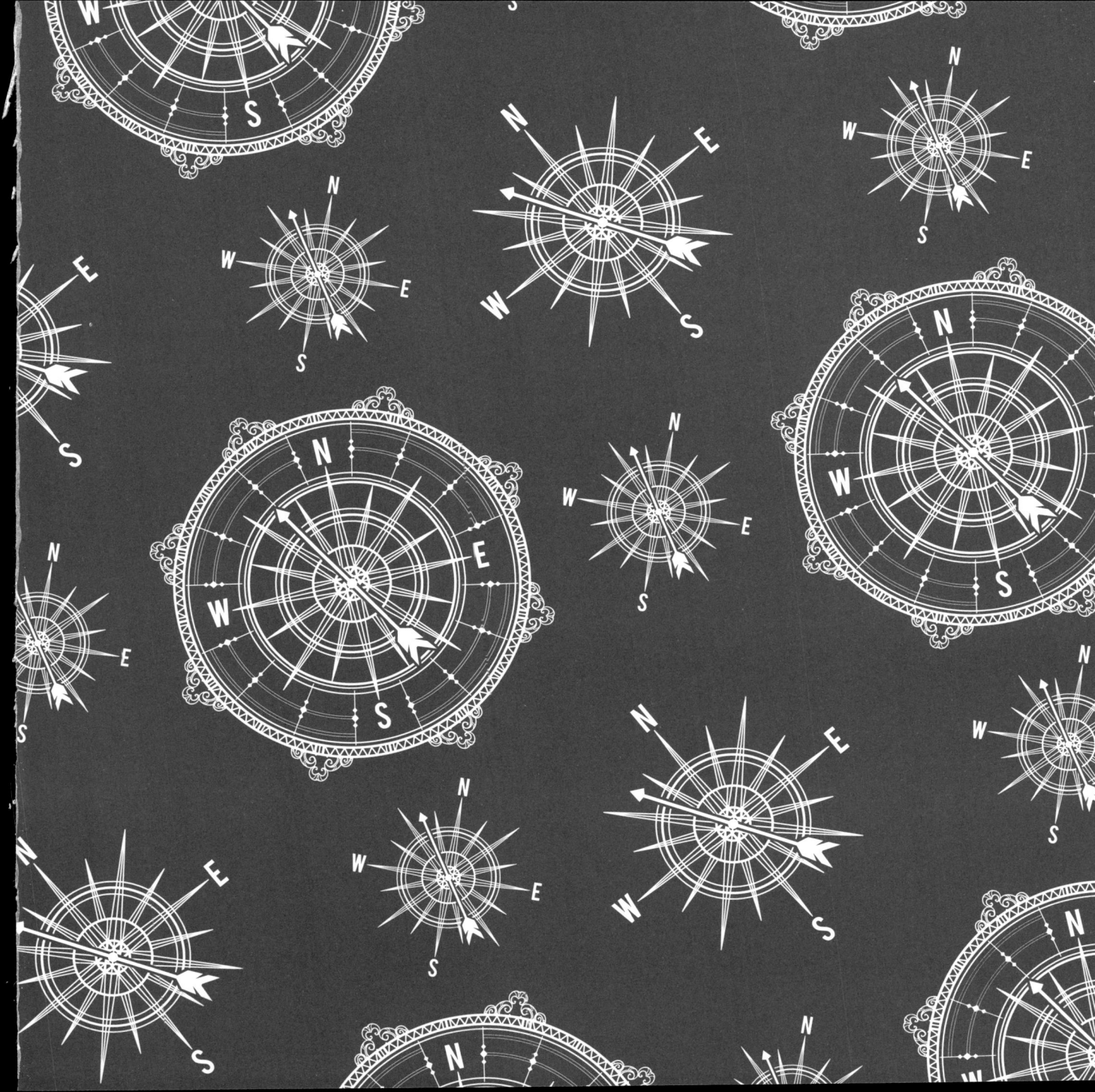

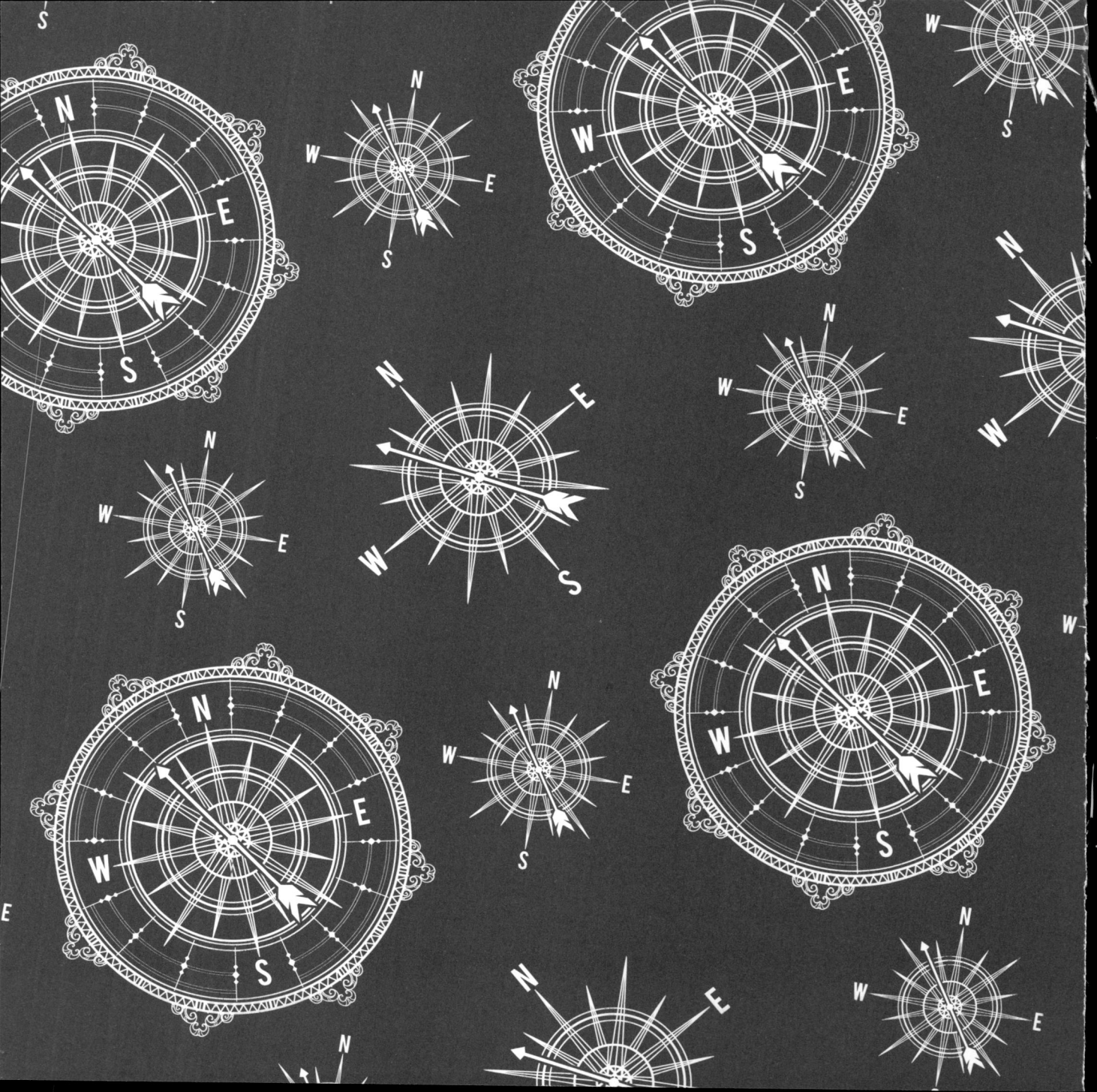